THE OLYMPICS

Peter Tatlow

The Bookwright Press
New York · 1988

Topics

Airports
Ancient Peoples
Archaeology
Bridges
Canals
Castles
Costumes and Clothes
Earthquakes and Volcanoes
Energy
Fairs and Circuses
Farm Animals
Ghosts and the Supernatural
Great Disasters
Helicopters
Houses and Homes
Inventions
Jungles

Language and Writing
Maps and Globes
Money
Musical Instruments
Peoples of the World
Photography
Pollution and Conservation
Prisons and Punishment
Railroads
Robots
Spacecraft
Television
The Age of Dinosaurs
The Olympics
Trees of the World
Under the Ground
Zoos

First published in the
United States in 1988 by
The Bookwright Press
387 Park Avenue South
New York, NY 10016

First published in 1987 by
Wayland (Publishers) Ltd
61 Western Road, Hove
East Sussex BN3 1JD
England

© Copyright 1987 Wayland (Publishers) Ltd

Library of Congress Catalog Card Number: 87–71053
ISBN 0–531–18183–9

Phototypeset by Kalligraphics Ltd, Redhill, Surrey
Printed in Belgium by Casterman S.A., Tournai

Cover: *The men's 800m at the 1984 Olympics in Los Angeles.*

All the words that appear in **bold** are explained in the glossary on page 30.

Contents

The Ancient Greek Games

The Olympic Games are held every four years in a selected country, and they are open to athletes of all nations.

The word Olympic comes from Olympia in Greece, where the ancient Games were always held. The first recorded Olympic Games were held in 776 B.C. and took place every fourth year after that date until they were abolished by a Roman emperor in A.D. 394.

An ancient vase depicting chariot racing, the most spectacular event of the early Greek Games.

Olympia was an open space around which stood a few buildings, mostly temples and shrines. The Games area – the **stadium** and **hippodrome** – was situated outside the walls of the holy enclosure.

The ancient Greeks worshiped many gods – they had one for nearly every aspect of life. Zeus, the supreme god, was in charge of thunderstorms and tempests. His temple was at Olympia, and the contestants swore their Olympic oath – to play fair – to him. Perhaps they hoped that he would provide good weather for the Games.

The ruins of the practice gymnasium at Olympia, used by the first Olympic athletes.

The first Olympic Games consisted only of a foot race of about 192m (200 yds), and the whole festival lasted one day. Later, the program became more varied, and five days were allowed, with many religious ceremonies being held in between the sports events.

Only men were allowed to take part in the events – women were banned. Chariot racing was the most spectacular event as the horses charged furiously around a

Boxing in the ancient Games was particularly vicious because the contestants wore spiked gloves.

circular course. The running races were more difficult than today because the athletes had to run in full armor. Horses were ridden bareback, without stirrups. Foot races ranged from 200m to nearly 5,000m. A five-fold event called the **pentathlon** consisted of discus and javelin throwing, standing long jump, wrestling and a short foot race.

The entrance to the sports stadium at Olympia.

The large crowd of spectators demanded excitement, and an event known as the *pancratium* gave them all the thrills they wanted. This was a brutal and

7

A reconstruction of Olympia showing the stadium and hippodrome where the ancient Games were held, and the Temple of Zeus in the background.

violent mixture of wrestling, boxing and judo, with punching, slapping and kicking allowed.

Winning first place in an event was the only glory in the ancient Games – second and third places were not recognized. The winners received a wreath made from the branches of the sacred olive tree and they also benefited from rewards such as good jobs and being excused from paying taxes.

The Modern Olympics

In 1894, after more than 1,500 years, Athens, the capital of Greece, was chosen for the site of the first modern Olympics. The Panathenean Stadium, built in 330 B.C., was reconstructed for the occasion. The founder of the modern Olympic Games was a Frenchman named Baron Pierre de Coubertin, who also founded the Olympic Committee and headed it until 1925.

The first Olympic Committee of 1925, founded by Baron de Coubertin (second from left).

After the successful 1896 Games in Athens, Greece wished to host them every time, but the Olympic Committee decided that each **Olympiad** should be held in a different country.

The following two Olympics, held in 1900 in Paris, and in 1904 in St. Louis, Missouri, were not successful. The events were spread over several months as mere sideshows to national exhibitions. Facilities were poor and the judges and officials lacked experience. The lesson learned from these disastrous

A painting of the start of the 100m at the 1896 Olympic Games.

The Chinese gymnast Li Ning is shown here on the pommel horse at the 1984 Los Angeles Olympics.

Olympics was that proper facilities were vital to the modern Games. In future, host countries had to provide good transportation and accommodation for competitors, and for the next Games, held in 1908 in London, the White City Stadium was especially built. Since then the facilities have improved with each Olympic Games.

The first Olympic village for competitors was built in Los Angeles in 1932. For the Tokyo Olympics of 1964, vast sums of money were spent on travel facilities, and a new underground railway was built in Munich for the 1972 Olympics.

Contestants in the Olympic Games must be **amateur** athletes. The range of sports increases with each Games but always includes the following summer sports: archery, athletics (track and field), basketball, boxing, canoeing, cycling, equestrian sports, fencing,

The exciting women's slalom at the 1984 Winter Olympics held in Yugoslavia.

football (soccer), gymnastics, handball, field hockey, judo, modern pentathlon, decathlon, rowing, shooting, swimming, diving, water polo, volleyball, weightlifting wrestling and yachting.

The **marathon**, first staged in 1896, commemorates the legendary feat of a Greek soldier, who carried news of victory from the battlefield at Marathon to Athens, a distance of 26 miles (41.84 km). The modern marathon was extended to 42.195 km at London in 1908. It was run from Windsor to London, and the extra distance was added so that it would start under the windows of the royal nursery at Windsor Castle. That distance was accepted as standard after a ruling in 1924.

The Winter Olympics, held in suitable alpine situations every four years, include such sports as skiing, bobsledding, figure skating, ice hockey, ski jumping, speed skating and tobogganing, or **Luge**.

One of the most dramatic events in the athletic stadium is the pole vault.

Thousands of balloons being released at the opening of the Los Angeles Olympics in 1984.

The opening ceremonies of both the Summer and Winter Olympics are very impressive. At the beginning of the Games, the Olympic flag is hoisted to a fanfare of trumpets, and pigeons and balloons are released. Then the Olympic flame, which has been carried from Olympia by a relay of runners, is carried into the stadium, and the Olympic torch is lit. After this the Olympic Hymn is sung and then a contestant from the host country pronounces the Olympic oath on behalf of all the athletes taking part in the Games.

The Olympic torch burns throughout the Games and is then extinguished at the closing ceremony. During the ceremony a moving speech is made, declaring that the flame will not be lit again until all the world's athletes are once more called together at the next Olympic Games – to be held in four years.

Olympic Golds

The first Olympic winner was Elian Koreobos, whose 192m (200 yds) sprint at Olympia in 776 B.C. won him an Olympic olive wreath. In 1896, a Greek shepherd, Spyridon Louis, won the first marathon, running 40 km (25 mi) in two hours, 58 minutes and 50 seconds. As a reward the King offered him any prize he wanted. He asked only for a horse and cart.

The first event winner in modern Olympics, was James Connolly of

The winner of the marathon in 1908, Dorando Pietri of Italy, was later disqualified because he was helped across the finishing line.

the U.S., for his triple jump of 13.71m. The U.S. also claimed the first Winter Games gold medal, for the 500m speed skating, won in 44 seconds by Charles Jewtraw. The event was held at Chamonix in the French Alps in 1924.

Sonja Henie, the exciting Nowegian skater at the 1932 Olympics. She later became a Hollywood movie star.

Johnny (Tarzan of the Apes) Weissmuller won seven gold medals for swimming, at the Paris Olympics in 1924, and again at Amsterdam in 1928, before going to Hollywood to make his career in films. In 1932, at St. Moritz in Switzerland, Sonja Henie from Norway won the figure skating title with an exciting performance on ice of the Dying Swan from the ballet *Swan Lake*.

In the Berlin Olympics of 1936, Adolf Hitler, the German Chancellor, expected Germany to win every medal possible for the glory of the Nazi regime. He was not pleased when Jesse Owens of the United States won the 100m, 200m and long jump. However Germany did win 33 gold medals against the United States 24.

At the Helsinki Games in 1952, Emil Zatopek of Czechoslovakia won the 5,000m, 10,000m and the marathon, and his wife Dana won

Abebe Bikila from Ethiopia was the first African Olympic winner and also the first competitor to win two consecutive marathons.

the gold medal for javelin throwing. Also at Helsinki, the Russians returned to the Games after a forty-year absence, to win the team and top individual gymnastics titles.

At the Rome Olympics in 1960, Ethiopia's Abebe Bikila won the marathon, running barefoot in a record two hours, 15 minutes, 16.2 seconds. In 1964, in Tokyo, he became the first man to win two consecutive marathons.

The delightful Russian gymnast Olga Korbut, thrilled audiences at the Montreal Olympics in 1976.

Britain's great athlete Daley Thompson won the decathlon in 1980 and 1984.

At Munich in 1972, Russia's Olga Korbut set the gymnastics world alight with her performances, and in Montreal in 1976, fifteen-year-old Nadia Comaneci from Rumania scored the first ten (a maximum score and a perfect performance) in Olympic gymnastics.

Britain's Daley Thompson set a new record by winning the **decathlon**, scoring 8,847 points at Los Angeles in 1984. Athletes who compete in the decathlon are amazing competitors – they have to

Daley Thompson is awarded the gold medal at the Los Angeles Olympics, once again beating his great rivals Jurgen Hinson and Heine Wentz of West Germany.

enter ten different events over two days and must score the highest number of points to win the event.

One of the unluckiest athletes must be Mary Decker of the United States, who missed Montreal (1976) through injury; Moscow (1980) because of an American **boycott**; and then, at Los Angeles (1984), tripped over Britain's Zola Budd and fell out of the 3,000m race.

The Olympics and the Wider World

In spite of many symbols of peace and friendship, sports frequently reflect the rifts and troubles between nations. In Ancient Greece, a truce to war was always declared during the Games, but this has not happened in the twentieth century – the Olympics were not held during the world wars of 1914–18 and 1939–45.

Adolf Hitler used the Berlin Olympics of 1936 to glorify his Nazi regime.

For various reasons, a few nations are usually absent from every Olympiad. Following the First World War, which ended in 1918, Germany, Austria and Japan were not invited, and neither were Germany nor Japan after the Second World War, which ended in 1945. Other difficulties have beset the Games. In 1936, Adolf Hilter used the Berlin Olympics for **propaganda** purposes, attempting to turn them into a glorification of his Nazi state.

A tragedy occurred in 1972 at the Munich Olympics, when Arab

Many countries boycotted the 1984 Los Angeles Olympics but this barely affected the sprints, where the U.S. athletes were supreme. Carl Lewis winning the men's 100m.

terrorists attacked the Olympic village and killed eleven Israeli athletes. In 1980, the United States, Germany and Japan stayed away from the Moscow Games, as a protest against the Russian invasion of Afghanistan. Then in 1984, Communist countries boycotted the Los Angeles Olympics for various reasons, including a fear of insufficient protection for their athletes.

Many people believe that elaborate Olympic ceremonies are becoming a showpiece for the host country rather than for the Games themselves.

The memorial service held to commemmbrate the athletes killed by terrorists at Munich in 1972.

Sad to say, the Olympic Games are severely threatened by political pressures. Because sports are internationally popular and receive a great deal of publicity in newspapers and on TV and radio, some countries use the Olympic Games to draw attention to political causes that might otherwise be overlooked.

The Future

The Olympic Games have changed greatly since the first modern Olympics were held at Athens. In 1896, only 13 countries competed, and all the contestants were men. Women first took part in the Games in Paris, four years later. By 1968, at the Mexico City Olympics, 112

The Olympic torch is lit at Olympia and carried across land and sea to light the Olympic flame.

25

countries and 5,530 contestants took part, 781 of them being women. In 1980, at Moscow, 1,088 women competitors entered.

When Baron Pierre de Coubertin revived the ancient Games in 1896, he believed that only good could come from having athletes of all countries of the world assemble once every four years to compete in friendly contests.

One symbol of world friendship in sports is the Olympic torch, which is lit at Olympia and carried through many countries – and sometimes by plane across oceans. Finally it is taken into the stadium and lights up the Olympic flame, which burns brightly in a bowl throughout the Games. Another symbol of world friendship is the Olympic flag of five colored rings linked together. The rings are blue, yellow, black, green and red. Every national flag in the world has at least one of these colors.

The Olympic flag of five colored rings and the Olympic flame – symbols of world friendship.

The U.S. runner Valerie Briscoe-Hooks winning the 400m at Los Angeles; like other athletes she spent years training for this event.

Olympic medals are highly prized by competitors who may train for many years for events that last only a few seconds. In ancient Greece, **professional** and amateur athletes competed together, and there was no Olympic prize money. There is still no prize money today, but unlike the ancient Games, the modern Olympics do not allow professionals to compete. Therefore, in order to be able to take part in the Games, competitors must put any money they earn from sports into a fund, which they may use only for training facilities or travel.

There are pressures on the Olympic authorities to admit professionals to the Games, but the aim of every professional athlete is to win. So such a step would change the entire concept of the Olympic

Windsurfing is one of the newest Olympic sports. Each Olympiad sees the introduction of new, exciting events.

Games. The following words are displayed on scoreboards at the opening ceremony of every Olympiad:

"The most important thing
in the Olympic Games is
not to win but to take part . . ."

These words express the hope that fair play and good sportsmanship will prevail throughout the Games.

Athletes train for many years in the hope of competing in the Olympics – the world's greatest sports contest and a lasting symbol of goodwill among nations.

Glossary

Amateur Someone who takes part in an activity, such as sports, as a pastime and not for financial gain.

Bobsledding Competition for men on a specially designed sled for two or more people. The sled can be steered, enabling it to be directed down a steeply banked ice-covered run.

Boycott To refuse to have dealings with. In this case, a refusal to attend the Games as a form of protest.

Decathlon Ten events for men over two days, with points awarded for every event. The events are: the 100m, long jump, shot putt, high jump, 400m, 110m hurdles, discus, pole vault, javelin and 1,500m.

Hippodrome An oval-shaped course for horse and chariot races in Ancient Greece.

Luge A small tobaggan, steered by ropes. Women as well as men compete in the luge event.

Marathon A foot race of 42.195 km – an event included in the modern Olympics.

Olympiad In Ancient Greece the four-year interval between the holding of the Olympic Games. Today, the staging of the modern Olympics.

Pentathlon A contest, for women only, consisting of five different events: 100m hurdles, shot putt, high jump, long jump and 800m – javelin and 200m added recently to make it women's heptathlon.

Professional Someone who makes a living from activities that are also performed by **amateurs.**

Propaganda The organized spreading of information to assist or damage the cause of a government or movement.

Stadium A sports arena. In Ancient Greece a course for foot races.

Books to Read

After Olympic Glory: The Lives of Ten Outstanding Medalists by Larry Bortstein. Warne, Frederick, & Co., 1978.

The Best Sports Book in the Whole World by Mauri Kunnas. Crown, 1984.

Careers in Sports by Bob and Marquita McGonagle. Lothrop, 1975.

Olympic Games in Ancient Greece by Shirley Glubok and Alfred Tamarin. Harper & Row Junior Books, 1984.

Olympics by Dennis B. Fraden. Childrens Press, 1983.

The Summer Olympics by Caroline Arnold, updated ed. Franklin Watts, 1988.

The Winter Olympics by Caroline Arnold. Franklin Watts, 1983.

Picture acknowledgments
The illustrations in this book were supplied by: Allsport front cover, 10, 11, 12, 13, 14, 15, 16, 17, 18, 19, 20, 21, 22, 23, 25, 26, 27, 28, 29; Mary Evans 9; Popperfoto 24, Ronald Sheridan Photo Library 4, 5, 6, 7, 8.

Index